Original title:
Pieces of Hope

Copyright © 2024 Swan Charm
All rights reserved.

Author: Aron Pilviste
ISBN HARDBACK: 978-9916-89-817-8
ISBN PAPERBACK: 978-9916-89-818-5
ISBN EBOOK: 978-9916-89-819-2

Emblems of Tomorrow

In the dawn's gentle light we see,
The whispers of hope, pure and free.
Every shadow fades with His grace,
Guiding our hearts to a sacred place.

Faith like a river, flows deep and wide,
Washing our burdens, we no longer hide.
With every tear, a promise anew,
The emblem of tomorrow shines bright and true.

Stars in the heavens, a divine decree,
Each one a blessing, a gift to thee.
In the silence, His voice we hear,
Calling us forth, quelling our fear.

Harvest our dreams with hands open wide,
Trust in the journey, let love be our guide.
Through valleys of doubt, we'll always prevail,
With faith as our compass, we'll never fail.

As the sun sets, we count our days,
In gratitude's light, we offer our praise.
For each moment lived, each prayer we share,
The emblems of tomorrow, a testament rare.

The Canvas of Tomorrow

With brushes dipped in light,
We paint the dawn anew.
Each stroke a whispered prayer,
Each hue a hope shines through.

In shadows of the dusk,
The future's glimmers spark.
Faith guides the hand of fate,
Transforming night to mark.

Amidst the trials faced,
The heart beats ever strong.
A vision forged in grace,
The canvas carries on.

With colors of the soul,
We weave a world of peace.
In unity we stand,
Our love will never cease.

Blossoms from Despair

In gardens filled with tears,
The rain brings gentle grace.
From sorrow's deepest roots,
Spring blooms in every place.

Hope nests in brittle leaves,
Defying winter's chill.
In darkness, seeds take hold,
Awaiting warmth to thrill.

The bud of faith emerges,
Rejecting barren ground.
In every heart's despair,
A joyful song is found.

With patience like the dawn,
We rise from depths of woe.
For every ache we feel,
A fragrant bloom will grow.

Lanterns in the Gloom

When shadows cloak the night,
And whispers fill the air,
Our lanterns shine so bright,
A beacon of our care.

Through trials faced alone,
We gather strength in prayer.
With light from hearts that yearn,
We banish every scare.

Each flicker sets a path,
For souls that wander near.
In unity, we stand,
Our visions crystal clear.

These lanterns, made of hope,
Will guide us through the dark.
Together in the light,
We find our sacred spark.

A Tapestry of Promise

Threads of faith intertwine,
In vibrant colors spun.
Each story, a design,
Of battles lost and won.

With every gentle stitch,
We weave our dreams as one.
A tapestry of love,
Embracing everyone.

In patterns of the past,
The future's bright and bold.
Each promise woven tight,
A legacy to hold.

Though life may fray at seams,
We clasp our hands in prayer.
Together we'll create,
A world beyond compare.

Songs of Seraphim

In the silence of the night,
The seraphim take their flight.
Whispers rise like fragrant bloom,
Singing praise beyond the gloom.

Wings of light through heavens soar,
Chanting love forevermore.
Voices blend in radiant grace,
Filling all the sacred space.

Echoes of the divine choir,
Hearts ignited by His fire.
In their song, the truth is found,
A harmony that knows no bound.

Resting in His warm embrace,
Every fear begins to chase.
Heaven's beauty, pure and bright,
Guides the lost back to the light.

As we join that heavenly sound,
In His mercy, we are bound.
Songs of seraphim we sing,
To the Lord, our offering.

Illuminated by Prayer

Beneath the stars, we gather near,
With hearts open and spirits clear.
Voices lifted, grace bestowed,
In the stillness, faith will grow.

Words like lanterns pierce the dark,
Filling souls with His sweet spark.
In shadows deep, the truth we find,
Illuminated, heart and mind.

Breath of life, our souls entwine,
In His presence, we align.
Every prayer, a sacred thread,
Woven through the lives we've led.

Hope arises, fears subside,
In His love, we will abide.
With each whisper, each ascent,
We find strength, our hearts content.

As dawn breaks, a promise shines,
In the silence, love defines.
Illuminated by His grace,
In His arms, we find our place.

The Promise of Dawn

As night yields to morning light,
Hope awakens from its plight.
With each sunrise, shadows fade,
In His love, our fears arrayed.

Nature sings a brand-new song,
In His arms, we all belong.
Every ray, a touch divine,
Guiding hearts through the entwine.

The promise of dawn brings peace,
In His mercy, fears will cease.
Through valleys deep, He leads the way,
Filling hearts with joy each day.

Every moment, grace unfolds,
In the warmth of love, we hold.
In the stillness, truth is found,
Hope eternal, hearts unbound.

With the sun, our spirits rise,
Heaven's plan before our eyes.
The promise of dawn renewed,
In His love, we are imbued.

Gentle Touch of Mercy

In the quiet, He draws near,
Every whisper calms our fear.
With a gentle touch, He heals,
In His love, our heart reveals.

Tears like rivers, He collects,
Embracing all our lived regrets.
With compassion, He restores,
Opening wide His heaven's doors.

In every trial, there's a grace,
Finding strength in His warm embrace.
When the world seems harsh and cold,
His mercy's warmth we shall behold.

Through the storms, His hand we seek,
In our weakness, He is meek.
Every burdensome yoke cast down,
In His mercy, we are crowned.

With each breath, His love we hold,
In the gentle touch, we're told:
Mercy flows like the sweetest stream,
Filling hearts with hope's bright beam.

Fragrant Longings

In gardens filled with grace and light,
We seek the blooms of love each night.
With hearts uplifted, we aspire,
To find the spark of holy fire.

Amidst the whispers of the breeze,
Our souls, entwined, find sweet release.
In every petal, every prayer,
We scent the longing everywhere.

From depths of silence, we arise,
Embracing faith that never dies.
Each fragrant breath, a soft caress,
In sacred moments, we find rest.

With longing hearts, we yearn to hear,
The echoes of the love so near.
In every shadow, light shall dwell,
In fragrant longings, all is well.

Attuning to the Divine

As morning dawns with golden hues,
We seek to embrace the sacred muse.
In tranquil moments, spirits soar,
Attuned to love forevermore.

With every breath, we feel the grace,
The rhythm of a holy place.
In whispers soft, the soul aligns,
Awakening to grand designs.

With open hearts, we lift our voice,
In unity, we make our choice.
To honor what the spirit brings,
In harmony, our hearts take wings.

In silent prayer, we find our way,
The light of hope will never stray.
Attuning deep to love divine,
In every heartbeat, we entwine.

The Revival of the Soul

From ashes, dreams shall rise anew,
In sacred space, the heart breaks through.
With healing light, we start to see,
The spirit's song sets us free.

In valleys deep, we find our strength,
In every challenge, God's great length.
The revival calls us to the flame,
In love's embrace, we find our name.

With courage born from deep within,
We shed the doubts, embrace the sin.
Revived in faith, we walk the path,
In joyfulness, we feel the wrath.

Through trials faced, we learn to grow,
In every wound, the light will show.
The revival whispers on the breeze,
In heartfelt moments, we find peace.

A Song of Surrender

In gentle waves, our spirits sway,
With every breath, we find our way.
In deep surrender, hearts unite,
A song of love shines ever bright.

To let go of the worldly chains,
We find the joy that ever reigns.
In trust, we place our lives in grace,
In all we are, we find our place.

With open hands, we seek to share,
A life of kindness, hope, and care.
In surrender sweet, we find our song,
Together, we are where we belong.

As dawn breaks forth with love's embrace,
We dance in joy, a sacred space.
A song of surrender lifts us high,
In unity, we touch the sky.

Ashes to Altars

From ashes we rise, seeking the flame,
Renewed in spirit, calling His name.
With every trial, our hearts engage,
Turning our sorrows into a sage.

From dust to dawn, we will ascend,
Building on faith, our souls we mend.
In every tear, a promise laid,
From brokenness, the light conveyed.

The altar we build is made of grace,
In every struggle, we find our place.
Sacred the journey, together we walk,
In whispers of love, our souls will talk.

With hands raised high, we seek the divine,
In unity's strength, our hearts align.
From ashes to altars, we make our stand,
In the name of love, forever hand in hand.

The Light Beyond Suffering

In shadows we wander, seeking the light,
Through valleys of anguish, we yearn for the bright.
His comfort surrounds, in silence we find,
The whisper of hope that frees the mind.

For every tear shed, a lesson unfolds,
In the crucible's fire, our spirits are bold.
We rise from the ashes, renewed and alive,
In the light of His promise, we learn to thrive.

The weight of our burdens, He carries each day,
Transforming our sorrow into praise we say.
Beyond the suffering, the joy is revealed,
In the arms of the Savior, our fate is sealed.

Through trials we journey, our faith grows strong,
In the darkest of nights, we sing our song.
With eyes turned to heaven, we trust in His plan,
The light beyond suffering holds out His hand.

Crystalline Moments

In crystalline moments, clarity shines,
When silence speaks truth, breaking the lines.
Each heartbeat a promise, a breath of the soul,
In fragments of time, we find ourselves whole.

Like dew on the grass, so tender and pure,
The grace of His presence, our hearts endure.
In every still instant, a whisper of peace,
In crystalline moments, our worries cease.

When life's storms are raging, we seek His embrace,
In such fleeting seconds, we witness His grace.
The beauty within every trial we face,
Crystalline moments, our spirits we trace.

With eyes wide open, we savor the now,
In gratitude's posture, we humbly bow.
For each breath of love, we lift up our voice,
In crystalline moments, together rejoice.

Heartbeats of Hope

With each heartbeat, a whisper of grace,
In rhythms of faith, we find our place.
The pulse of creation, in unity flows,
In heartbeats of hope, our spirit grows.

Through trials we face, we rise and we stand,
Embracing the journey, hand in hand.
In shadows and light, His love interweaves,
In heartbeats of hope, the faithful believe.

Each moment a treasure, each breath a gift,
In silence we gather, our spirits lift.
For every heartbeat, a promise is spoken,
In love's gentle embrace, no heart is broken.

Through nights of despair, we will not lose sight,
For hope is our lantern, guiding the light.
In heartbeats of hope, we shall carry on,
In the arms of His mercy, we are reborn.

Chasing Celestial Dreams

In the hush of night we seek,
Guided by stars, softly we speak.
Heaven's whispers call our name,
With faith ablaze, we'll fan the flame.

Through trials and shadows, we tread,
With hope in hearts, where angels led.
A tapestry of light unfurls,
Woven with love, transcending worlds.

The path may waver, winds may shift,
Yet souls unite in a sacred gift.
As prayers ascend on wings of grace,
In every heartbeat, we find our place.

With every tear, a lesson learned,
In every joy, a heart discerned.
Through valleys low and mountains steep,
In faith, we sow the dreams we keep.

Together we rise on wings of prayer,
Chasing the light, banishing despair.
In eternal quest for the divine,
Chasing celestial dreams, we shine.

The Dance of the Faithful

In the quiet morn, we gather here,
With every step, the clouds draw near.
Hands uplifted, voices raised,
In rhythm of love, we are amazed.

The earth beneath, the sky so wide,
With hearts entwined, we walk beside.
Each twirl a message, pure and clear,
In the dance of the faithful, we persevere.

As candles flicker in the night,
Each flame a vow, a spark of light.
Together we move, we bend and sway,
In the warmth of grace, we find our way.

With every leap, a new beginning,
In joyful hearts, the faith is spinning.
As heavens open, blessings fall,
In the dance of the faithful, we stand tall.

So let us dance till daylight breaks,
In praise of love, our spirit wakes.
With every beat, our souls align,
In this sacred dance, forever divine.

Alight with Aspiration

In the dawn there shines a beam,
A promise bright, a sacred dream.
With hearts alight, we take our stand,
Embracing grace with open hands.

Each morning brings a chance anew,
With whispered hope, our spirits grew.
On paths of faith, we tread with care,
In the light of love, we learn to share.

When shadows fall and doubts arise,
We lift our gaze to endless skies.
With every prayer, a star takes flight,
Through darkest nights, we seek the light.

With strength in unity, we rise,
In every challenge, see the prize.
Bound by conviction, fierce and strong,
We march together, hearts in song.

Alight with aspiration, we proclaim,
In every heartbeat, we fan the flame.
With souls ignited, we'll journey on,
In faith united, we cannot be gone.

Notes from the Heavens

In silence deep, the heavens sing,
A melody of hope, on gentle wing.
With every note, our spirits soar,
In harmony, we seek much more.

The stars above, they flicker bright,
Each twinkle shares a sacred light.
Notes from the heavens, soft and clear,
Guide us onward, year by year.

In the garden where dreams do bloom,
We nurture love, dispel all gloom.
The whispers echo, soft yet strong,
In unity, we find where we belong.

With every prayer, a song takes flight,
A testament to faith's pure might.
In the melody of the divine,
We hear the notes, forever entwined.

As day transforms and shadows play,
We cherish each moment, come what may.
In these notes of love, we rejoice,
Together, we rise, in one strong voice.

Radiant Echoes of Tomorrow

In dawn's embrace, hope softly stirs,
Whispers of grace dance on the air.
Heaven's light, a guiding flame,
Illuminates paths, redeeming our name.

With every step, faith we ignite,
Carving our dreams into the night.
Blessed are we in trials faced,
Through love's embrace, we find our place.

In the beauty of nature's song,
The echoes of tomorrow linger strong.
With every heartbeat, we rise anew,
A promise of life, vibrant and true.

A Heartbeat Amidst the Silence

In the stillness, a heartbeat sings,
A whisper of love that gently clings.
Silent prayers lift to the skies,
In the quiet, our spirit flies.

Among the shadows, light breaks through,
Hope's gentle hand in all we do.
Each moment cherished, faith extended,
In depths of silence, love is blended.

In solitude's arms, fears dissipate,
Finding solace in the hands of fate.
The pulse of grace, forever near,
A heartbeat of peace, our vision clear.

Fragments of Faith

In pieces scattered, dreams reside,
A tapestry woven, time and tide.
Each fragment shines with purpose true,
A symphony of life, in every hue.

From ashes rise, a sacred fire,
Rekindled hope, our hearts inspire.
Through storms we journey, hand in hand,
Faith's unbeaten path, forever grand.

With every trial, strength bestowed,
In brokenness lies the love we sowed.
Together we heal, together we stand,
In fragments of faith, united we band.

Shards of Light

Through shattered glass, the sun cascades,
Casting rainbows where darkness fades.
In every shard, a story speaks,
Fractured beauty that life seeks.

A montage of hope, a light divine,
Picking up pieces, hearts intertwine.
Each sparkle ignites the night unknown,
Bringing warmth to every heart, your own.

In the chaos, grace unfolds,
In every shard, a truth retold.
We rise from darkness, finding our way,
In shards of light, come what may.

A Thread of Healing

In quiet prayers, we find our way,
Through threads of grace, both night and day.
With gentle whispers, love abides,
In every heart, the Spirit guides.

Each wound we bear, a story told,
A tapestry of faith, pure gold.
In unity, we rise above,
Bound by the thread, entwined in love.

The hands of time may seem to fray,
Yet hope remains, come what may.
For healing flows in sacred streams,
Awakening our truest dreams.

The light breaks forth, a dawn so clear,
In moments still, we cast out fear.
With every breath, we learn to see,
The thread of healing, holding free.

The Still Waters of Faith

Beside the still waters, peace awaits,
In quietude, the Spirit creates.
A gentle current, soft and sure,
In faith, our hearts find hope so pure.

The trials come, like storms at sea,
Yet faith remains, our trust shall be.
With every wave that rises high,
We seek our strength, and learn to fly.

Reflecting now, on waters deep,
In moments still, our souls we keep.
Beneath the surface, life runs free,
In faith's embrace, eternally.

With open hearts, we journey on,
The light of faith, our guiding dawn.
In stillness found, we learn to see,
The waters flow, and set us free.

The Embrace of the Unknown

In shadows deep, we find our way,
The unknown calls, we dare to stay.
With every question, whispers rise,
We seek the truth beyond the skies.

A journey bold, we make alone,
In faith's embrace, we find our home.
The mysteries unfold with grace,
In every breath, we find our place.

Step by step, we walk the path,
Through trials faced, we seek His wrath.
Yet in the dark, a light shines bright,
The embrace of love, our guiding light.

With hearts aflame, we yearn to know,
The beauty found in trials' flow.
Trusting the journey, come what may,
In the unknown, we learn to stay.

Journeying Toward the Light

With every dawn, a path unfolds,
In journeying, our hearts grow bold.
Toward the light, we walk with grace,
Embracing each and every space.

Through winding roads, we find our song,
In faith, united, we belong.
The shadows fade as we pursue,
The promise found in love so true.

Each step we take, a testament,
To the journey's beauty, heaven-sent.
In trials faced, we rise and stand,
Together bound, hand in hand.

With joy we carry, hope aflow,
In every heart, the Spirit grows.
Journeying forth, with souls alight,
We find our way, toward the light.

Fragments of Joy

In the quiet morn, grace descends,
Whispers of love, the heart amends.
Like sunbeams dancing on the dew,
Each moment a gift, ever true.

In laughter shared, the spirit soars,
A gentle nudge from heaven's doors.
With every smile, a fragment shines,
In unity, our joy aligns.

Through trials faced, faith takes its stand,
With open hearts, we clasp God's hand.
In fragments small, His light reveals,
The boundless love that always heals.

In gratitude, we raise our voice,
In harmony, we make our choice.
Embracing life, with all its grace,
Finding joy in every place.

So let us gather, hand in hand,
In the sacred circle we will stand.
Together, in peace, we'll find our way,
In fragments of joy, we shall stay.

Illuminated Paths

Where shadows creep, and doubts arise,
Look to the light that never dies.
In every step, the Spirit calls,
Guiding us through life's winding halls.

With muddy roads and stones to face,
Find strength in faith, and hope's embrace.
Every challenge, a chance to grow,
In illuminated paths, we'll go.

Through valleys deep and mountains high,
In quiet moments, hear the sigh.
The universe speaks in whispers sweet,
In holy cadence, our souls meet.

Embrace the dawn, let worries flee,
For in the light, our souls are free.
With open hearts, we wander forth,
Seeking the treasures of our worth.

Together we walk, hand in hand,
In love's embrace, we firmly stand.
With stars above, our spirits throng,
On illuminated paths, we belong.

Starlit Horizons

As twilight weaves its silken thread,
Dreams awaken, the heart is fed.
Under the sky where starlight gleams,
We find the truth within our dreams.

In silent prayer, our hopes take flight,
Guided by faith through the night.
Each star a promise, shining bright,
Whispers of heart in the still light.

With every step, we seek the heart,
In unity, we'll never part.
Together we face the night's embrace,
Seeking the light in every space.

Through cosmic fields where wonders dwell,
Each breath we take, a sacred spell.
In starlit horizons, we shall sing,
Of love and light, eternally spring.

So lift your gaze, let courage rise,
For in the dark, our spirits prize.
In starlit paths, our dreams unfold,
A journey of grace, forever bold.

A Journey Beyond Shadows

In the silence where shadows loom,
Hope ignites in the heart's warm room.
Each step we take, a whisper shared,
In faith, we walk, a love declared.

Through valleys deep and mountains wide,
With hearts united, we will abide.
Each trial faced, a chance to soar,
A journey beyond, forevermore.

Through stormy seas and skies of gray,
In search of truth, we'll find our way.
As dawn breaks forth, the shadows flee,
With every breath, we shall be free.

In moments frail, let love prevail,
Our spirits lift; we will not fail.
Together, guided by the light,
We venture forth into the night.

So trust the path, and walk it bold,
For every story must be told.
In journeys vast, our spirits shine,
Beyond the shadows, love divine.

The Sanctuary Within

In silence dwells the sacred light,
A heart that sings through darkest night.
With whispered prayers and gentle grace,
We find our refuge, a holy place.

Within the soul, the spirit thrives,
A haven where the true one strives.
Amidst the chaos, peace shall reign,
With faith's embrace, we break the chain.

Each moment spent in quiet thought,
Unveils the truth that love has wrought.
The sanctuary, our most dear,
Where all are safe, and none must fear.

Beneath the stars, with open eyes,
We witness grace that never dies.
As prayers ascend like gentle streams,
We touch the essence of our dreams.

So let your heart be ever still,
Invite the light to bend your will.
In sanctuary, we find the way,
To walk in love, to live, to pray.

Echoes of the Eternal

In whispers soft, the truth resounds,
Where ancient wisdom still abounds.
Through time and space, the echoes call,
Reminding hearts to rise, not fall.

The rivers flow with tales untold,
Of faith and love, both strong and bold.
Each step we take, the path reveals,
A sacred bond that time conceals.

In shadows cast by ages past,
The voice of spirit is unsurpassed.
With open hearts and listening ears,
We find the strength to conquer fears.

The stars above, companions bright,
Guide us forth through darkest night.
In every heartbeat, there's a song,
An echo to which we all belong.

Embrace the stillness, breathe it in,
Let faith renew our strength within.
Eternal whispers lead the way,
To realms where love shall always stay.

Serene Anchors

In the storm's eye, we find our peace,
With anchors deep that never cease.
The weight of love shall hold us fast,
Through trials faced, our faith will last.

Each moment served, a sacred gift,
In gentle hands, our spirits lift.
Amidst the waves, we turn in prayer,
For in His light, we're always there.

The calm that flows within our hearts,
Gives courage when the tempest starts.
With every breath, His promise stays,
A guiding star through murky ways.

When doubts arise like raging seas,
We anchor down, find strength with ease.
Through trials faced, our souls shall soar,
With faith as anchor, evermore.

Together, bound by love's own thread,
We walk in grace where angels tread.
For in this life, with hearts aligned,
Serene anchors, our souls entwined.

A Garden of Favor

In gardens lush where hopes arise,
With fragrant blooms beneath clear skies.
The seeds of faith we plant each day,
In gentle earth, they find their way.

With tending hands, we nurture grace,
In every shadow, light we trace.
The blossoms speak in colors bright,
Of love's embrace and purest light.

A tapestry of life unfolds,
In each small act, a story told.
Through trials faced, we learn to sow,
The seeds of love, that always grow.

Amidst the thorns, we find our way,
Embracing joy, come what may.
For every tear helps others bloom,
In this vast garden, there's always room.

So let your heart be soft and pure,
In favor's garden, we shall endure.
Together, hand in hand, we stand,
In grace we thrive, across this land.

Crumbs of Comfort

In shadows deep, where hearts do dwell,
A whisper of peace, a sacred spell.
Soft crumbs of grace, by mercy shared,
Each morsel reminds us, we are prepared.

With every sigh, our burdens lighten,
In faith's embrace, the heart ignites,
From trembling lips, a prayer ascends,
Hope woven tight with love that mends.

Together we gather, in spirit bound,
In the aching silence, comfort found.
Though trials come, we stand as one,
United in grace, till day is done.

The smallest acts, like seeds of light,
Illuminate paths in darkest night.
Each crumb a reminder, we are not alone,
A banquet prepared, where love is sown.

In gratitude we walk, through valleys low,
Hand in hand, as the soft winds blow.
For in each crumb, a promise thrives,
Our souls entwined, our spirits rise.

The Manna of the Spirit

From heavens high, the blessings rain,
Manna of spirit, in joy and pain.
Each drop a lesson, each grain a call,
To rise in faith, and never fall.

In desert places, where shadows creep,
A feast of love that nourishes deep.
With open hands, we gather the day,
Finding sustenance in prayer's soft sway.

The spirit dances on whispers sweet,
In every heartbeat, we find our feet.
Blessings flow like a gentle stream,
Awakening hope, igniting the dream.

In every moment, a chance to see,
The miracles hidden, so softly free.
With each new dawn, we rise anew,
In the manna of spirit, pure and true.

So let us share this heavenly bread,
In love's embrace, where angels tread.
With every morsel, grace will expand,
Together in unity, we take a stand.

Seeds of Serenity

In quiet gardens, we plant our seeds,
Whispers of peace, the heart now leads.
With tender hands, we nurture the earth,
From chaos born, we find our worth.

Every moment, a breath divine,
In stillness found, the holy design.
Rays of sunlight through branches sway,
Guiding our spirits along the way.

As storms may come and shadows pass,
These seeds of serenity forever last.
Roots intertwined in love's embrace,
In every challenge, we find grace.

Through seasons change, our faith to grow,
With each dawn, endless beauty to show.
In unity strong, we rise as one,
Harvests of love, when day is done.

So let us flourish, in peace abide,
With seeds of serenity as our guide.
Together we bloom, in heavenly light,
In gardens of faith, we take flight.

Remnants of Rebirth

From ashes born, we rise anew,
Remnants of rebirth, a sacred view.
Each scar a story, each tear a tale,
In the dance of life, we shall prevail.

With hope revived, our spirits soar,
In gentle whispers, we hear the lore.
The past may linger, but we press on,
In the dawn of grace, we're never gone.

The cycle turns, with seasons bright,
In every challenge, a guiding light.
Together we walk, in faith's embrace,
Finding our strength in love's own face.

Through trials faced, we find our voice,
In every moment, we shall rejoice.
Remnants of rebirth, shining clear,
A symphony of hope, we hold dear.

So let the journey lead us home,
In unity's strength, we shall not roam.
For every ending brings forth new grace,
In the remnants of rebirth, we find our place.

Treasures in the Trials

In the shadows, faith is found,
Gold emerges from the ground.
With each struggle, lessons bloom,
Whispers of hope break the gloom.

Patience shapes the weary soul,
In brokenness, we become whole.
Each tear shed a sacred sign,
A heart refined through love divine.

Through storms of doubt, a light appears,
Guiding us through all our fears.
In trials we learn to abide,
With grace, our burdens cast aside.

The path of thorns leads to grace,
In every trial, we find our place.
Emerging stronger from the pain,
In sacred trust, we rise again.

For every tear and every sigh,
An angel's whisper from on high.
Treasures lie in hearts that ache,
With love's embrace, we will awake.

The Hopeful Flame

In darkest night, a flicker glows,
A gentle warmth that ever flows.
Hope ignites in weary hearts,
A flame that never shall depart.

Through trials faced, the fire grows,
Casting light where doubt bestows.
Faith's embrace, a guiding hand,
Through every storm we boldly stand.

Even when the winds may howl,
Within, the sacred embers grow.
With each breath a prayer ascends,
The hopeful flame that never ends.

In moments still, we find our peace,
With every struggle, doubts decrease.
This flame within shall light the way,
A promise bright, come what may.

And as the dawn begins to break,
The world awakens, hearts partake.
We share the flame, our spirits soar,
Together, love forevermore.

Signs Along the Journey

Along the path where shadows blend,
We seek the signs that love extends.
In whispered breezes, hearts will hear,
The gentle call that draws us near.

Each step we take, a sacred dance,
In every moment, a second chance.
Through mountain highs and valley lows,
The guiding light of truth still glows.

In silence deep, the soul will speak,
The signs appear for those who seek.
With open hearts, we learn to see,
In every trial, divine decree.

A fluttering leaf, a starry night,
The world reveals its sacred light.
In nature's voice, the truth unfolds,
A tapestry of love retold.

So journey on with faith so bright,
The signs will lead us through the night.
In every moment, grace we find,
With open hearts and open minds.

Pathways to the Sacred

Each step we take upon this ground,
Leads to the love that's all around.
In every breath, the spirit dwells,
In whispered prayers, the heart compels.

Through valleys deep and mountains high,
We walk in faith, we reach for sky.
With every heartbeat, grace we seek,
In humble service, His voice speaks.

The sacred paths twist and weave,
In love's embrace, we learn to believe.
Through trials faced, our faith will grow,
In every moment, divinely flow.

With eyes wide open, hearts aligned,
Together, we shall seek and find.
The pathways lit by love's own fire,
In every soul, the sacred choir.

As dawn renews the weary day,
We walk together, come what may.
The journey unfolds in sacred time,
Forever wrapped in love's sweet rhyme.

Springs of Joy in Arid Lands

In deserts bare, where shadows lie,
Faith's whisper calls, a gentle sigh.
From rocky soil, blooms rise anew,
The heart's delight, in morning dew.

When burdens weigh and hope seems dim,
His light shines bright, our hearts to brim.
With every step on this dry ground,
Springs of joy in Him abound.

Through trials fierce, we find our way,
Guided by love, we kneel and pray.
In arid lands, His grace restores,
Our weary souls, forever yours.

Each dawn we greet with thankful song,
In His embrace, we all belong.
With every tear, a lesson learned,
From ashes rise, our spirits burned.

So let us dance, though storms may rage,
With faith as our strength, we turn the page.
For in His hands, we are made whole,
Springs of joy, refreshing soul.

Echoes of Sanctuary

In quiet halls where prayers resound,
Lost souls find peace, their hearts unbound.
With every hymn, a gentle grace,
The echoes call to seek His face.

In shadows deep, His light will shine,
A fortress built, so pure, divine.
With each soft word, our fears retreat,
In sanctuary, our hearts then meet.

Through trials faced and sorrows shared,
A loving voice, forever bared.
In every heart, His truth abides,
In echoes soft, His love provides.

Together bound, we share this space,
In His embrace, we find our place.
With lifted hands and voices high,
We sing of joy that will not die.

The sanctuary stands forever strong,
In every note, we sing along.
With thankful hearts, we rise and stand,
In echoes true, we touch His hand.

Wings of the Spirit

Upon the breeze, the Spirit flies,
In gentle winds, our fears arise.
With every breath, His presence dear,
Our hearts awaken, drawing near.

With wings of hope, we soar above,
In all our trials, wrapped in love.
Through valleys low and mountains steep,
In faith, we walk, His promise keep.

In sacred spaces, whispers true,
The Spirit guides in all we do.
Through storms that rage and skies so gray,
He lifts our hearts, our fears array.

With every moment, grace unfolds,
In courage found, the brave and bold.
As wings of light, our spirits sing,
In unity, together bring.

So let us fly, with hearts aligned,
In every journey, love enshrined.
From earth to sky, our souls unite,
On wings of spirit, we take flight.

Harvests of Grace

In fields of gold, the harvest waits,
With open arms, love celebrates.
Through toil and tears, we sow each seed,
In patience firm, we trust His lead.

As seasons turn, the bounty grows,
In every heart, His mercy flows.
Through trials faced, our spirits bloom,
In faith we find our hearts' perfume.

With gratitude, we gather round,
The fruits of labor, grace abounds.
Each blessing shared, a gift divine,
In every bond, His love entwine.

Through laughter shared and kindness shown,
In every prayer, we're never alone.
With thankful hearts, we lift our praise,
For harvests gathered, life's brightays.

So let us tend this sacred ground,
In every moment, He is found.
In unity, our hearts embrace,
For in our lives, we reap His grace.

The Horizon of Belief

In the dawn's embrace, hope takes flight,
Whispers of grace break through the night.
Each soul seeks light, a path divine,
As stars align in their sacred design.

The mountains stand with steadfast pride,
Guardians of dreams, where hearts confide.
In valleys deep, our spirits soar,
To the horizon of belief, we implore.

With hands uplifted, we seek our way,
Through trials faced, we humbly pray.
The journey long, yet faith ignites,
A beacon bright in the darkest nights.

The whispers echo in sacred space,
Every heartbeat sings of grace.
In the quiet stillness, we find our peace,
In unity's bond, our doubts release.

On this sacred path, we walk with trust,
In love's embrace, we rise from dust.
Together we stand, hearts intertwined,
In the horizon of belief, we're aligned.

Vessels of the Divine

We are vessels strong, created to hold,
The love of the heavens, pure and bold.
In every trial, our spirits blend,
With mercy flowing, hearts to mend.

From ancient texts, wisdom flows,
In humble prayer, the spirit glows.
Through storms we weather, with courage bright,
Guided by faith, we seek the light.

Each life a tapestry, woven with care,
In every moment, a chance to share.
With kindness offered, the world we embrace,
As vessels of the divine, we find our place.

In silent reflection, we hear the call,
To cherish each gift, both great and small.
With gratitude swelling, we rise and sing,
For in loving service, true joy we bring.

Through trials faced, our bond grows tight,
In unity's glow, we're wrapped in light.
Together we stand, a beautiful sign,
As living testaments, vessels divine.

Flickers of Faith

In the twilight hours, a flicker ignites,
A dance of shadows, a promise of sights.
Through doubt's haze, a spark appears,
Flickers of faith dissolve our fears.

In sacred moments, prayers take flight,
On whispered winds, they reach the height.
United in spirit, our hearts will race,
Finding our strength in the quiet place.

With every heartbeat, hope springs anew,
In flickers of faith, we see what's true.
Through valleys low and mountains high,
We feel the presence, we know the why.

As stars emerge from the cloak of night,
So does our faith in the boundless light.
With hands extended, we share the glow,
Flickers of love in the world below.

Together we rise, as shadows retreat,
In the warmth of faith, we hold our seat.
For in this journey, with hearts aligned,
Flickers of faith, our souls entwined.

Mysteries of the Blessed

In the folding of time, secrets arise,
Mysteries of the blessed, beneath the skies.
Each moment whispers of sacred grace,
In the fabric of life, we find our place.

With eyes wide open, we search for truth,
In the laughter of children, the fire of youth.
Through trials faced, and burdens shared,
The mysteries unfold, as love is declared.

In quiet reflection, the soul takes heed,
For every heart carries a beautiful seed.
To nurture with kindness, and watch it grow,
In the mysteries of the blessed, we come to know.

As the dawn breaks, unveiling the day,
We step into light, casting shadows away.
The journey unfolds with wisdom profound,
In mysteries of the blessed, our peace is found.

Together we gather, in circles of grace,
Embracing the lessons, time won't erase.
In unity's song, our spirits soar free,
In the mysteries of the blessed, we shall be.

Radiance in the Ruins

In the shadows where hope seems lost,
Light breaks through, a divine cost.
Amidst the ashes, whispers arise,
Promising grace, the soul's prize.

Each step forward, the heart's embrace,
Guided by love, the truest grace.
From crumbling stones, new paths unfold,
A story of faith, in silence told.

Through trials met, we learn to see,
The hidden strength of unity.
In every crack, a seed will bloom,
Turning despair into room.

The spirit soars, unbound, set free,
In ruins, we find our destiny.
Radiant echoes, forever bright,
Illuminate the darkest night.

Together we rise, hand in hand,
In the rubble, we firmly stand.
With every heartbeat, a call to rise,
In radiant love, no more disguise.

Threads of Redemption

Woven gently through life's seam,
Threads of mercy form a dream.
Each challenge faced, a lesson learned,
In the fire of faith, our spirits burned.

In every tear, a story spun,
Of battles fought, and victory won.
Through darkest nights, the dawn will break,
With threads of grace, our lives remake.

Though we falter, we seek the light,
Hand in hand, we face the night.
The tapestry grows, in colors bold,
Of love and hope, and truths retold.

In moments sweet, and bitter too,
A sacred path we walk anew.
For in each heart, a prayer resides,
A beacon strong, where love abides.

Threads of redemption, intertwined,
A promise true, divinely designed.
Together we weave, with spirits free,
An endless journey, eternity.

Embers of Eternity

From the ashes of what once was,
Rise the embers, soft and splayed.
Carried on winds of whispered prayer,
In every heart, a spark laid bare.

The flames of hope, they flicker still,
Promising warmth, a sacred thrill.
Through trials faced, our souls ignite,
In the darkness, we seek the light.

Each moment cherished, a gift bestowed,
The path to grace, steadily showed.
In unity, we build anew,
Embers glowing, forever true.

With every breath, we recognize,
The beauty found in each sunrise.
Through fleeting time, our spirits soar,
Embers of love, forevermore.

In the quiet, hear the call,
Embers dance, they rise and fall.
Each flicker holds a sacred tale,
Of faith enduring, we will prevail.

Beneath the Veil of Tears

Beneath the veil, where sorrows dwell,
Lies a heart that speaks, a silent bell.
In every drop, a story flows,
Of love and loss that deepens grows.

Through weeping skies, our hopes ascend,
In grief, we find the strength to mend.
The whispers soft, a gentle hand,
Guiding us to a promised land.

In the darkest hours, light will break,
With every tear, a soul awake.
Embracing pain, we learn to heal,
The sacred truth, so deeply real.

For in the hurt, we find the way,
To brighter tomorrows, come what may.
Beneath the veil, a light will shine,
Reminding us, our hearts align.

With every tear, a prayer we weave,
In sorrow's depth, we shall believe.
For love remains, through pain and fears,
Eternal joy beneath the tears.

Fragments of Divine Light

In shadows deep where hope may wane,
A flicker shines, a soft refrain.
Hearts seek the glow, a path to find,
In fragments bright, He weaves the blind.

Each ray a promise, pure and sweet,
A guiding spark where lost souls meet.
The echoes call, the spirits rise,
In divine light, the truth belies.

Through trials faced, we learn to see,
The gift of grace, from Him to me.
With every tear, the heavens weep,
In light's embrace, our faith runs deep.

Awake, arise, let joy abound,
In every heart, His love is found.
Through fleeting moments, sacred sights,
We gather all in His soft light.

These fragments rare, each shining hue,
A testament of love so true.
In unity, our spirits shine,
As fragments blend, His light divine.

Whispers of Grace in the Shadows

In silence deep, where shadows play,
The gentle whispers guide our way.
Through trials harsh, His voice we hear,
In every doubt, He holds us near.

A breath of grace, where faith does stir,
In moments still, His heart does purr.
The unseen truths, like stars they gleam,
Through darkest nights, we chase the dream.

With every heartbeat, hope's refrain,
In whispers soft, He breaks our chains.
Though storms may rise and winds may roar,
In grace we stand, we fear no more.

Each flicker bright, a sign of love,
From realms beyond, from heights above.
In shadows cast, His light will dance,
In whispers sweet, we find our chance.

So let us heed that sacred sound,
In every step, His grace is found.
With open hearts and eyes that see,
In whispered grace, we are set free.

Beyond the Brokenness

In cracks of soul, where pain resides,
Hope glimmers forth, where love abides.
Through struggles faced and burdens borne,
We find the path, through night to morn.

The scars we wear, a tapestry,
In brokenness, we find the key.
Each fragment holds a story dear,
In healing arms, we'll shed our fear.

With hands outstretched, we seek the peace,
In every tear, our grief's release.
Beyond the hurt, where joy awaits,
In faith's embrace, our spirit debates.

Together we rise, through trials clear,
In unity, we cast out fear.
For every wound, a sacred grace,
In brokenness, we find our place.

Through every tear, we glimpse the light,
In shadows deep, we find the sight.
Beyond the broken, we are made whole,
In love's embrace, we nurture the soul.

Morsels of Faith

In every heart, a morsel small,
A seed of faith, though frail, stands tall.
In quiet moments, strength we find,
As whispers speak from the divine.

Each crumb a gift, in trials faced,
A taste of hope, in coils laced.
With open hands, we share the feast,
In unity, our souls released.

Though storms may rage and doubts may creep,
In faith we trust, no promise sleeps.
For every morsel shared with grace,
Transforms the world, our sacred space.

The journey long, with paths unknown,
Each step we take, we find a home.
In every morsel, love's embrace,
Sustains our spirit, quickens pace.

Together we rise, in faith we soar,
Through tiny bites, we hunger for more.
In morsels shared, His light we see,
In every heart, He sets us free.

The Soft Embrace of Belief

In shadows deep, a whisper calls,
Faith rises strong, where darkness falls.
An open heart, a humble plea,
Guided by love, we long to see.

Together we stand, hand in hand,
A dream unfolds, by hope we land.
Through trials faced, we find our way,
In trust's soft arms, we choose to stay.

In sacred moments, we find grace,
With every tear, a warm embrace.
The soul ignites, a gentle spark,
Illuminating the deepest dark.

When doubt arrives, we turn to prayer,
A quiet breath, a sacred spare.
The light within, we won't forsake,
In faith's embrace, no fear can break.

So lift your voice, let praises rise,
In every heart, God's love complies.
Together we'll journey, steadfast and true,
In the soft embrace, we are anew.

Tiny Triumphs

In every dawn, a chance to grow,
Small victories, gently flow.
A kind word shared, a smile so bright,
In tiny triumphs, we find our light.

The humble acts, they may seem slight,
Yet in them shines the purest light.
A helping hand, a stranger's cheer,
In these moments, God feels near.

With each small step, the heart expands,
Love's gentle touch, in unseen hands.
Through trials faced, we rise with grace,
Tiny triumphs, our sacred space.

A child's laughter, a soft embrace,
In every heartbeat, God's sweet trace.
The world transformed by love's sweet dance,
In tiny triumphs, we take our chance.

Moments of Divine Intervention

In silent prayer, a call to Him,
In darkest hours, when hopes grow dim.
A gentle touch, a whisper clear,
Moments of grace, dispelling fear.

The hands of fate, they intertwine,
Guided by love, a plan divine.
In every tear, a lesson learned,
Through trials faced, our spirits burned.

When paths are crossed, and souls align,
In woven threads, His love will shine.
Intervened by faith's sweet hand,
In every heart, His promises stand.

We find our strength in love's embrace,
In moments rare, we see His face.
Through endless time, we rise above,
Moments divine, wrapped in love.

A Crown of Light

The journey long, through valleys low,
With every step, our spirits grow.
A crown of light, awaits us true,
In faith, we rise, with hearts anew.

Through trials faced, we seek His face,
In every storm, we find our place.
With courage bold, we stand as one,
A legacy of love begun.

He whispers hope in darkest night,
Guiding us gently toward the light.
The road may twist, but hearts align,
A crown of glory, truly divine.

In every struggle, we find our song,
In the arms of love, we all belong.
Lifted above, with spirits bright,
Together we wear, our crown of light.

starlit paths of Belief

In shadows deep, the stars do gleam,
Guiding hearts along the stream.
With faith as light, we walk the night,
On starlit paths, our souls take flight.

Each step we take, a prayer in air,
In whispered hopes, we cast our care.
The heavens wide, a map divine,
In unity, our spirits entwine.

Through trials faced, our hearts remain,
In love's embrace, we rise again.
With every spark, a promise bright,
Together bound by sacred light.

The journey long, yet never lost,
In faith we find the strength it costs.
Our starlit paths, forever true,
Illuminate the way anew.

In sacred trust, we seek the way,
With every dawn, a brand new day.
Embrace the light, dispel the fear,
For in our hearts, the truth is clear.

The Soul's Resilience

Amidst the storms that life may send,
The soul stands strong, it shall not bend.
In darkest hours, a light will shine,
Resilience blooms, through grace divine.

The weight of trials, heavy it seems,
Yet from the ashes, rise our dreams.
With every fall, the spirit grows,
In silent strength, true courage shows.

Through tears and joy, the path we tread,
The whispers of hope, by angels led.
In every heartbeat, a story told,
Of faith unshaken, of love untold.

In sacred moments, we find our peace,
With every prayer, the worries cease.
A tapestry woven, with threads of grace,
The soul's resilience, our sacred space.

With open hearts, we rise together,
In unity strong, no storm can tether.
Through trials faced, our spirits soar,
The soul's resilience, forevermore.

Lighthouses of Aspiration

In the distance, bright towers stand,
Guiding us gently, hand in hand.
With beams of hope, they light the way,
In lighthouses bright, our dreams hold sway.

Through turbulent seas, we navigate,
Drawn by the light, we contemplate.
With courage strong, we heed the call,
Aspiration shines, reminding us all.

Each flicker bright, a promise near,
In moments dark, we conquer fear.
Our hearts aligned, we sail as one,
In every storm, the battle's won.

With steadfast faith, we plant the seeds,
Of love and hope, fulfilling needs.
In lighthouses' glow, we find our way,
Transforming night into the day.

Across the tides, our spirits rise,
Chasing the light beneath vast skies.
For every dream, in hearts we keep,
Lighthouses of aspiration, wide and deep.

Doves of Renewal

In sacred skies, the doves take flight,
Bearing our dreams, in gentle light.
With wings outstretched, they soar above,
Whispering tales of peace and love.

From troubled times, their presence brings,
A soothing balm, as hope it sings.
Each flutter soft, a promise made,
In every heart, despair will fade.

In circles drawn, they dance with grace,
Uniting souls in a warm embrace.
With every coo, a song we share,
A vision bright, a world laid bare.

Through dusk and dawn, they glide along,
A symphony of spirit, pure and strong.
In moments still, our fears release,
As doves of renewal bring us peace.

So let us rise, with wings anew,
In every heart, the dove shines through.
To heal the world, we must believe,
In doves of renewal, we receive.

Echoes of Grace

In the stillness of the night,
The heart seeks a guiding light.
Whispers of mercy in the air,
Gentle reminders of love and care.

Grace descends like morning dew,
Renewing all that's tried and true.
In every trial, solace flows,
In every sorrow, healing grows.

Faith unfurls like a gentle breeze,
Lifting the weary, granting ease.
In shadows deep, the spirit sings,
Embracing hope that comfort brings.

Love's embrace, a sacred song,
In unity, we all belong.
Through the valleys, we traverse,
Echoes of grace, in every verse.

With every step, the path is clear,
In every heartbeat, God is near.
Through pain and joy, the soul awakes,
In life's embrace, each spirit takes.

Whispers from the Divine

Softly spoken, truths divine,
In moments still, the stars align.
Every breath a sacred prayer,
Whispers of love linger in the air.

In the longing hearts ignite,
A silent flame, a guiding light.
With every dawn, a promise near,
In every shadow, faith draws near.

Listen close, the spirit's call,
In the quiet, fears do fall.
Like a river, grace will flow,
In the depths of the heart, we grow.

Angels dance on the winds of change,
In their presence, lives rearrange.
Hope returns, like morning sun,
Whispers of peace, when day is done.

Each soul a thread in the grand design,
Connected to the source divine.
Through every trial, love will find,
A way to heal, to be entwined.

Threads of Belief

Weaving dreams with every prayer,
Threads of belief, hanging in the air.
In obscured paths, light reveals,
The truth beneath, the heart reveals.

Every tear, a seed of grace,
In the garden of faith, we find our place.
With every struggle, the spirit grows,
In every doubt, a love still glows.

Binding hearts with threads so fine,
In unity, the souls align.
Through trials faced, we stand as one,
In the tapestry of life, God's work is done.

Through the storms, our spirits soar,
In the promise of faith, we seek for more.
The echoes of love surround our way,
In the fabric of grace, we find our stay.

With every heartbeat, a tale unfolds,
In the warmth of belief, our spirit holds.
Threads of hope in the loom of time,
In every verse, a purpose sublime.

Rays of Redemption

In the dawning light, forgiveness blooms,
Rays of redemption chase the glooms.
Every sorrow finds its peace,
In the heart's embrace, all worries cease.

Through valleys shadowed, the spirit glows,
In every trial, the truth bestows.
With gentle hands, we mend the seams,
Awakening life in forgotten dreams.

Shattered lives find healing grace,
In the warmth of love, they find their place.
With each sunrise, burdens fade,
In unity, the scars are laid.

Eclipsed no more, the soul takes flight,
In every shadow, a guiding light.
Through tears of joy, the heart expands,
In the rays of redemption, life withstands.

So lift your gaze to the skies above,
Embrace the light, the gift of love.
With every breath, let hope reside,
In redemption's embrace, we abide.

The Soul's Resilience

In shadows deep, we find our light,
Each trial faced, a sacred fight.
From ashes rise, the spirit sings,
In faith, we trust, on Hope's soft wings.

With storms that rage, we stand so tall,
Embracing grace, we heed the call.
Forged in fire, the heart refined,
In unity, our souls aligned.

The path is long, yet strong the stride,
With every step, our fears subside.
In whispers soft, the truth prevails,
As love releases all the veils.

In silence found, the strength appears,
A bond unbroken through the years.
For in His hands, our spirits dwell,
Through every storm, we rise and swell.

A tapestry, so richly spun,
With threads of mercy, we are one.
Together, in this sacred dance,
We find within, our true expanse.

The Quiet Offering

In stillness waits the heart's pure prayer,
A gentle breath, a whispered care.
In simple acts, His love we share,
The quiet offering, answered there.

The morning sun, so warm and bright,
Brings forth the promise of the light.
Each moment spent in presence bold,
A tale of grace, quietly told.

With every smile we choose to spread,
Our silent vows in kindness led.
The hands that serve, the hearts that mend,
In love's embrace, we find our friends.

Through trials faced, we seek the peace,
In humble hearts, our fears release.
For in the quiet, we discern,
The lessons taught, the love we earn.

With each new dawn, we rise anew,
In gratitude, our spirits grew.
In every choice, the truth bestowed,
A quiet offering, life's rich road.

Hourglasses of Grace

In hourglasses, time drips slow,
Moments captured, seeds we sow.
With every grain, a tale unfolds,
In grace we find what love beholds.

The present waits, a sacred trust,
In fleeting time, we learn how to adjust.
Each breath, a gift from Him above,
In every tear, He wraps His love.

As shadows blend with morning's glow,
We seek the paths where spirits flow.
For in the stillness, wisdom lies,
Awakening dreams beneath the skies.

With every glance, the heart reveals,
The pulse of life, the touch of heals.
In gentle moments, grace bestowed,
A journey deep, into His road.

Through hourglasses, we're called to dance,
In rhythms divine, we find our chance.
For every second holds a space,
To weave the fabric of His grace.

A Symphony of Redemption

In harmony, our hearts confess,
A symphony of sweet distress.
With every note, a story told,
Of love's embrace, of courage bold.

Through trials faced, we hear the chords,
Of timeless grace, our gentle Lord.
For in the darkness, light ignites,
A melody of pure delights.

With each refrain, our spirits soar,
United strong, forevermore.
In grace's rhythm, we unite,
A symphony of pure delight.

So let us sing, our voices blend,
In every heart, He will transcend.
For in our song, redemption found,
A love so deep, forever bound.

In sacred tunes, our souls will thrive,
In every beat, our spirits rise.
Together, we will find our way,
A symphony of love we play.

Lanterns in the Dusk

In twilight's glow, the lanterns sway,
Guiding hearts along the way.
Whispers soft from stars above,
Remind us all of boundless love.

Each flicker tells a sacred tale,
Of journeys vast, where spirits sail.
In shadows deep, the light shall stand,
A beacon bright, hand in hand.

The dusk, a canvas, painted wide,
With hopes and dreams, where souls abide.
Together, we shall find our grace,
In every smile, in every space.

The night shall come, but fear not strife,
For lanterns burn—an endless life.
Within their flame, we reignite,
The love that guides us through the night.

Tapestries of Tranquility

In silence woven, threads of peace,
Life's tempests calm, and troubles cease.
Each moment, stitched with tender care,
A tapestry, unique, laid bare.

With colors bright, our spirits sing,
In love's embrace, the joys we bring.
Every heart, a piece of art,
In unity, we never part.

The gentle breeze, a sacred hymn,
Whispers soft, where hope begins.
We walk together, side by side,
In tranquil fields, our hearts abide.

With hands entwined, we lift our prayer,
For harmony, a world so rare.
In every thread, divine design,
A spark of grace, forever shine.

The Seeds of Tomorrow

In fertile ground, we plant the seeds,
Of faith and love, of noble deeds.
Each whispered wish a tender plea,
To nurture hope in hearts, set free.

The rain shall fall, and sun shall shine,
As roots entwine, in purpose divine.
Gathering strength from soil below,
Together, we shall watch them grow.

With patience, we unveil each bloom,
A promise kept, dispelling gloom.
In every petal, beauty sings,
Of brighter days and wondrous springs.

So let us sow, with open hands,
In unity, where love withstands.
The seeds we plant, to bear the fruit,
Of kindness rich, a world to suit.

Celestial Cadence

Beneath the stars, a rhythm flows,
The universe in stillness glows.
In every pulse, a sacred beat,
Draws us closer, hearts in fleet.

The moonlight dances, soft and bright,
Enfolding dreams in gentle light.
In harmony, our spirits rise,
A symphony of endless skies.

With every breath, we join the song,
Of love and hope, where we belong.
In cosmic grace, we find our way,
A journey blessed, day by day.

Our souls entwined in rhythm's embrace,
A sacred dance, a boundless space.
In celestial cadence, we shall stand,
United, guided by His hand.

Chasing the Divine Whisper

In quiet prayer, my heart does seek,
A whisper soft, the words I dare.
With open soul, I yearn to hear,
The sacred call, the truth laid bare.

Through woven paths of faith I tread,
Each step a dance, a fleeting grace.
The spirit moves, divine and led,
In silence found, I find my place.

Beneath the stars, the heavens glow,
With every breath, I feel the light.
In darkness deep, the embers grow,
A beacon bright, dispelling night.

In moments soft, I find the lore,
Of ancient tales, the light of yore.
A whisper stirs, the heart's encore,
In sacred hush, forevermore.

Blossoms of Solace

Amidst the thorns, a bloom appears,
A testament to grace and hope.
In pain and strife, through all my fears,
The petals chant, in faith I cope.

Each morning dew, like tears of joy,
The sun bestows its gentle kiss.
In nature's arms, my heart's employ,
A sacred peace, a fleeting bliss.

In every flower, a prayer unfolds,
As colors merge in fragrant air.
The beauty speaks in tales retold,
Of love divine, a holy prayer.

Embrace the blooms that life extends,
Through joy and loss, in every hour.
In solace found, the spirit mends,
And blossoms rise, a sacred power.

Reflections in Sacred Waters

By waters deep, I cast my gaze,
The ripples dance, as if they know.
In liquid glass, my soul ablaze,
A mirror holds the light's soft glow.

Each droplet speaks of love and pain,
In tranquil depths, the truths reside.
Through flowing streams, the spirit's reign,
A current strong, my heart's guide.

With every wave, the whispers call,
In sacred rhythms, they align.
The echoes rise, and softly fall,
A chorus pure, the realm divine.

As twilight dims, the waters gleam,
In quiet calm, I find my rest.
Reflections show the sacred dream,
A journey blessed, my spirit's quest.

The Light that Endures

In shadows cast by worldly toil,
The light breaks forth, a guiding star.
Through darkest nights, the hearts uncoil,
For grace abides, no matter how far.

The flicker bright, a sacred flame,
In every soul, a spark divine.
With faith's embrace, we praise His name,
The light that leads, our hearts entwined.

Through trials faced, and storms that rage,
The light remains, a steadfast friend.
In every turn, we turn the page,
The love that lasts will never end.

Together we rise, both meek and bold,
In unity our spirits soar.
The light of hope, in hearts we hold,
Is life and love, forevermore.

Wings of Tranquility

Upon the hills where silence dwells,
The spirit soars, and peace compels.
In nature's arms, our worries cease,
A gentle touch, a whispered peace.

The river flows, a sacred song,
Reflecting love, where we belong.
With every breath, the soul takes flight,
In harmony with endless light.

The stars above, a guiding choir,
Igniting hearts, igniting fire.
With trust, we rise, in grace we find,
Wings of tranquility, pure and kind.

In prayerful hearts, we seek the way,
To walk in faith, each blessed day.
With each step, the path unfolds,
In quietude, our truth beholds.

So let us soar on heaven's breeze,
With fervent love that grants us ease.
For in this grace, we find our wings,
Embraced by all the joy it brings.

The Light Breaking Dawn

In darkness deep, the shadows fade,
A promise whispers, hope displayed.
As stars retreat with morning's grace,
The light breaks forth, a warm embrace.

Each beam of sun, a sacred stream,
Unveiling truths within the dream.
With every rise, a chance to see,
The path of light is meant to be.

The sky ignites with colors bold,
A tapestry of stories told.
In the dawn's glow, hearts intertwine,
Awakening to love divine.

With every dawn, our spirits soar,
As joy unfolds, forevermore.
In light we trust, our fears released,
In gratitude, we find our peace.

So let us dance in morning's grace,
Embracing life, a sacred place.
For light breaks forth with every day,
Guiding us on our chosen way.

Resonance of Truth

In stillness found, the heart will speak,
A song of hope, both strong and meek.
With every word, a power grows,
The resonance of truth, it flows.

Through trials faced and lessons learned,
In honest light, the spirit yearned.
To seek the way, to find the path,
With open hearts, we conquer wrath.

In unity, our voices rise,
A chorus bright beneath the skies.
With faith as our unwavering guide,
Together we will turn the tide.

Each whispered prayer, a bridge we build,
With love and grace, our hearts fulfilled.
In truth, we stand, both brave and strong,
As we embrace where we belong.

So let us live, our truth displayed,
In kindness shown and fears obeyed.
For in our hearts, the truth remains,
A melody that forever reigns.

Letters to God

With pen in hand, my heart laid bare,
I write to You, in humble prayer.
Each word a wish, each line a plea,
In letters sent, I long to see.

Through trials faced, I seek Your light,
In shadows deep, to find what's right.
Grant wisdom's gift, and love's embrace,
Let hope abound in every space.

In moments lost, I feel Your grace,
As whispers guide me in this race.
With gratitude, I seek to know,
The path You plan, where I shall go.

In joy and pain, I send my words,
As prayers take flight, like gentle birds.
In faith I trust, Your love will lead,
Through every doubt, through every need.

So here I stand, my heart exposed,
In letters sent, my love enclosed.
With every breath, I send my soul,
To You, dear God, make my heart whole.

Gentle Reminders of Grace

In the stillness of night's embrace,
Whispers of love touch my face.
Life's burdens I gently release,
Finding solace in sweet peace.

Each dawn's light brings hope anew,
Faith ignites the spirit's view.
In every heart, grace takes flight,
Guiding us through darkest night.

The mountains may rise, skies may weep,
Yet in His arms, I find my keep.
With every breath, His love restores,
Gentle reminders of open doors.

Through trials faced, with courage grand,
His guiding hand, a steady hand.
In gratitude, I rise and sing,
Celebrating each little thing.

For in each moment, blessings flow,
Seeds of love in hearts we sow.
With grace as our unending guide,
Together in faith, we shall abide.

Navigating Through the Abyss

In shadows deep where whispers dwell,
I seek the light, I know so well.
Amidst the storm, my heart will roam,
Finding strength, I call it home.

The waves may crash, the winds may roar,
Yet faith will open every door.
With steady steps, I face my fears,
Trusting the path, dry all my tears.

A beacon shines within the night,
Guiding souls towards the light.
In every trial, a lesson learned,
Through darkest paths, my spirit burned.

In silence deep, I find my peace,
As burdens lift and sorrows cease.
With love as compass, hope my sail,
Through every storm, I shall prevail.

For in the depths, my faith does bloom,
As grace will always find its room.
Together we shall journey far,
Navigating by heaven's star.

Seraphic Whispers

In twilight's hush, a soft refrain,
The seraphs sing, a sweet domain.
Their voices lift, like gentle light,
Embracing hearts, dispelling night.

Each note resounds, a call to grace,
Inviting all to seek His face.
In every breath, a sacred song,
Seraphic whispers, where we belong.

Through trials faced and burdens bare,
Their melodies climb through the air.
With open hearts, we shall comply,
For in their song, our spirits fly.

Finding peace in sacred hum,
The promise near, the hope to come.
Within the chorus, joy does swell,
A glimpse of heaven, all is well.

With every tear, a note set free,
Boundless love, our melody.
Together, joined in sacred cheer,
Seraphic whispers, drawing near.

Raindrops of Renewal

Softly they fall, the raindrops pure,
Each one a promise, a hope secure.
In every drop, a blessing flows,
Nurturing life, as love bestows.

They break the silence of parched earth,
Bringing forth joy, a vibrant birth.
In gentle rhythm, they dance and play,
Cleansing our souls as we find our way.

With every storm, a chance to grow,
In rain's embrace, faith starts to glow.
A canvas fresh, painted anew,
Life's sacred journey, ever true.

As rivers swell and flowers rise,
Hope blossoms forth beneath the skies.
Raindrops fall, a heavenly sign,
Healing our hearts, making us shine.

So let us gather, hearts entwined,
In raindrops of grace, joy we find.
Together we rise, ever anew,
In love's embrace, forever true.

Petals of Prayer

In whispered hopes, the heart unfolds,
Like petals gentle in the breeze.
Each prayer a note, a song untold,
Carried forth with sacred ease.

Beneath the branches, shadows dwell,
Where spirits dance in light divine.
With every breath, a story to tell,
In the stillness, the holy aligns.

Hands lifted high, we seek the grace,
To mend the world, to heal the pain.
In every tear, His warm embrace,
Hope blossoming like joyful rain.

In the silence, we find our way,
Through trials deep, through tempests wide.
A garden grows where faith can play,
In love we trust, in truth we bide.

So let the petals fall and soar,
In unity, our souls entwined.
With every prayer, we seek once more,
The blissful peace, the love defined.

The Blessing Beneath the Ashes

From burnt offerings, new life will rise,
In shadows thick, the light will gleam.
Through trials faced, God hears our cries,
And brings forth hope, a whispered dream.

Under the weight of sorrow's sigh,
Their embers glow, a radiant spark.
Faithful hearts will learn to fly,
In the darkness, there leaves a mark.

Every tear a sacred stream,
Washing pain from weary souls.
In every wound, a path to beam,
As grace bestowed makes broken whole.

In the ashes, a promise lies,
To rise again, to breathe anew.
From suffering's depths, the spirit flies,
In love's embrace, we find what's true.

So let us gather, hand in hand,
To find the blessings hidden here.
Together we will take our stand,
In every heart, His love draws near.

Glimmers of Salvation

The morning breaks with gentle light,
A promise shines upon our way.
In every heart, a spark ignites,
To guide us through both night and day.

With whispered words and kindness shown,
We find our path in love's embrace.
In every soul, the seeds are sown,
A garden blooms in sacred space.

Though storms may rage and shadows loom,
Hope flickers bright within the dark.
In unity, we dare to bloom,
As souls unite to leave a mark.

From doubt and fear, we seek release,
Together in this holy quest.
In glimmers found, we find our peace,
In faith and grace, we are blessed.

May every moment echo sweet,
The melody of life divine.
With open hearts, we shall repeat,
Our song of love, forever shine.

Sounds of the Sacred

In the hush of dusk, the world aligns,
The melody of grace unfolds.
With every breath, His love entwines,
A symphony of tales retold.

The rustle of leaves, a whisper sweet,
As nature's choir serenades.
With hearts awake, we lift our feet,
To dance along where fervor sways.

The distant chimes of hope resound,
In every pulse, a spirit glows.
As echoes rise from hallowed ground,
The light of faith within us grows.

So let the sacred sounds arise,
In laughter, tears—a joyous blend.
With open hearts, we hear the cries,
To love, to heal, to comprehend.

Together, we are one resound,
In harmony, our souls will find.
In every heartbeat, peace is found,
In every note, love intertwined.

Rays of Promise in the Gloom

In shadows deep, His light breaks through,
A guiding star, steadfast and true.
Whispers of hope in the heart's silent night,
Bathe us in grace, oh, heavenly light.

Through trials we walk, hand in His hand,
With faith as our shield, we firmly stand.
Each tear we shed, a seed of His love,
Rays of promise sent from above.

Mountains may tremble, oceans may roar,
Yet in His arms, we fear no more.
The tempest may churn, the skies may weep,
But His gentle voice bids our hearts keep.

In moments of doubt, we find our peace,
With every breath, His blessings increase.
Hope springs eternal, bright as the morn,
In the gloom of night, our spirits reborn.

Lifted by faith, on wings we rise,
Transcending the whispers, the worldly ties.
Rays of promise, shining divine,
In the depths of despair, forever we twine.

A Covenant of Comfort

In tenderness wrapped, we come to pray,
Seeking His shelter, our debts to pay.
For every burden, His love shall bear,
A covenant of comfort, a bond so rare.

Through valleys of sorrow, His hand leads on,
Each step unwavering, until the dawn.
With every heartbeat, His presence remains,
Healing our spirits, calming our pains.

His voice like thunder, yet gentle and near,
Calls us to stillness, casts out all fear.
In moments of trial, our refuge He is,
A sanctuary of peace, our eternal bliss.

With promises woven like threads of gold,
His love engraves what the heart can hold.
In silence we gather, a chorus of grace,
In a covenant sweet, we find our place.

As shadows retreat, our spirits unwind,
In His embrace, true solace we find.
Together we journey, hand in His hand,
A covenant of comfort, forever we stand.

Dances of the Devout

In circles of joy, the faithful meet,
With hearts ablaze, they lift their feet.
A melody sweet, the spirit's tune,
In dances of worship, we are made new.

Spinning in faith, they twirl and sing,
In the light of His love, their praises ring.
Each step a prayer, a sacred call,
In the dance of devotion, we give our all.

Hands raised to heaven, as souls entwine,
Each rhythm echoing the love divine.
In joyous abandon, they move as one,
In the dances of the devout, life's battles are won.

With every heartbeat, the passion flows,
In the warmth of His grace, true freedom grows.
Together we sway, in harmony's grace,
A tapestry woven, in love's embrace.

Let the music rise, let the spirit soar,
In the dance of the faithful, we ask for more.
In this holy rhythm, we're lost and found,
In dances of the devout, heaven bounds.

Chains Loosed by Love

In shadows cast by sorrow's chains,
Love's gentle hand breaks all our pains.
With every whisper, He calls us free,
Chains loosed by love, our spirits decree.

Hearts once burdened find light anew,
In love's embrace, our courage grew.
For every heartache, a lesson learned,
Through trials endured, our passions burned.

With open arms, He draws us near,
In the depth of love, we lose all fear.
From ashes of grief, we rise and sing,
As chains dissolve, our souls take wing.

Together we stand, through thick and thin,
United in love, we find our kin.
With faith as our guide, we journey forth,
In chains loosed by love, we find our worth.

In every heartbeat, His promise thrives,
In the light of His love, we feel alive.
Chains once binding, now lie in dust,
For love is our strength, our everlasting trust.

The Guardian's Embrace

In shadows deep, where whispers dwell,
A sacred light begins to swell.
With arms of faith, we find our way,
The Guardian guides us through the day.

Through valleys low, in trials faced,
His love, a warmth, our hearts embraced.
No fear shall grasp, no doubt remain,
In His presence, we break the chain.

With every breath, His mercy flows,
In gentle grace, our spirit grows.
A beacon bright, through darkest night,
The Guardian's hand, our guiding light.

In every tear, a blessing shared,
For weary souls, He has prepared.
A promise whispered, soft and clear,
The Guardian walks, forever near.

Awake, O heart, and rise anew,
In faith we stand, in love so true.
Embrace the light, let shadows cease,
For in His arms, we find our peace.

Fruits of Faith in Drought

In barren lands, where hope seems lost,
Faith's seeds are sown, regardless of cost.
Each leaf unfurls, against the odds,
In silent prayers, we meet our God.

The sun may scorch, the winds may roar,
Yet hearts believe, and spirits soar.
With gratitude, our voices rise,
In drought, we see life's sweet surprise.

From rocky soil, the fruits will bloom,
In direst times, God brings the loom.
He weaves our heartaches into grace,
A testament of love's embrace.

With every tear that drops like rain,
New life emerges from the pain.
In trials faced, our faith will shine,
A bounty rich, through love divine.

So let us plant with hearts aflame,
In desert's heat, we call His name.
For even in the strife we face,
We bear the fruits of His sweet grace.

Sunrise after the Storm

When tempests rage and shadows fall,
The dawn will break, peace conquers all.
With every wave that crashes down,
A brighter day will wear the crown.

In storms of doubt, we seek His face,
And find our refuge in His grace.
With every heartbeat, trust will rise,
As light peeks through the greyened skies.

The colors burst, a tapestry,
A promise made of hope set free.
Renewed, we stand, our hearts aglow,
For every storm must cease to flow.

In quiet moments, stillness reigns,
With faith we break the binding chains.
From every loss, a lesson learned,
The sunrise comes, our hearts now turned.

So praise the skies, for storms will pass,
In every heartache, joy will amass.
With open arms, we greet the morn,
For in His love, our lives reborn.

The Sower's Gentle Hand

With tender touch, the sower stands,
Casting seeds upon fertile lands.
In faith he plants, with hope ablaze,
Trusting in God through all our days.

Each grain of love, a story told,
In every hand, the hand of old.
Through trials faced, the heart will grow,
In patience learned, our spirits flow.

As seasons change and winds may shift,
The sower knows, God gives the gift.
With watchful eye, he breathes and waits,
For blooms of faith, the heart elates.

In rocky soil and shadows cast,
He nurtures dreams, in love steadfast.
Through storms of doubt, he storms the night,
To see the dawn, a world of light.

So let us sow, with hearts sincere,
In every loss, draw love near.
For in our hands, a future grand,
We trust in God, the sower's hand.

Gardens of Serenity

In the stillness of dawn, we find grace,
Whispers of heaven, in every place.
Faith blooms gently, with each soft prayer,
In gardens of serenity, love laid bare.

Under skies painted with divine light,
Hearts gather courage to face the night.
Petals of hope in the winds do soar,
Guided by angels, forevermore.

The path is winding, yet filled with peace,
In nature's embrace, our burdens cease.
With every tear, the earth does revive,
Here in His presence, our spirits thrive.

Sweet scents of mercy drift through the air,
We walk with purpose, unburdened care.
Each step a blessing, each moment a gift,
In gardens of love, our souls uplift.

Let joy be the harvest, a promise true,
Nourished by kindness, in all we do.
In the stillness of dawn, His light we see,
In gardens of serenity, we are free.

The Unseen Hand

In shadows where silence speaks His name,
An unseen hand guides us, without shame.
Through trials that challenge our weary souls,
He lifts us gently, and makes us whole.

Waves crash around, but we stand strong,
In whispers of faith, we know we belong.
His fingers weave peace in each trembling heart,
From darkness to light, He plays His part.

In moments when doubt tries to steal our light,
The unseen hand reaffirms our fight.
With every heartbeat, a promise we trace,
In valleys of struggle, He shows His grace.

When burdens feel heavy, and skies are gray,
His presence surrounds us, come what may.
In stillness, we feel Him, a gentle embrace,
Our fears dissipate, in His boundless space.

So trust in the hand that leads us back home,
Through journeys unknown, we are never alone.
In love everlasting, our souls intertwine,
With the unseen hand, forever divine.

A Prayer Unfurling

In the quiet of night, a prayer does bloom,
Petals of hope dispel all the gloom.
Whispered confessions, like stars in the sky,
Rise to the heavens, where angels reply.

Each breath a promise, each sigh a plea,
In the tapestry woven, we find our key.
With faith as our anchor, our worries depart,
A prayer unfurling from a humble heart.

Like rivers of grace, our voices will flow,
Through valleys of sorrow, we nurture the glow.
In shadows of doubt, let courage ignite,
With a prayer unfurling, we embrace the light.

In the stillness we gather, our spirits unite,
With offerings of love, our burdens take flight.
In moments of silence, our truths come to be,
A prayer unfurling, setting the spirit free.

So let us be vessels of mercy and care,
With each prayer offered, we lighten the air.
In kinship with angels, our voices will sing,
A prayer unfurling, to Him we bring.

Vined Hope in Parched Soil

In parched soil we wander, searching for rain,
Roots of our longing dive deep into pain.
Yet hope is a vine, that grows ever near,
In the warmth of His love, we harbor no fear.

Through cracks of despair, life bravely will creep,
A testament strong, in the promise we keep.
Each drop from the heavens, a blessing bestowed,
Fortifying faith, as our spirits explode.

With every small bud that breaks through the ground,
We find strength in unity, together we're found.
The vine wraps around, holding hearts close,
In the garden of trials, His love is the most.

In whispers of hope, our laughter does rise,
With eyes lifted high, we see through the skies.
Against all the odds, we blossom and grow,
For within us all, lies a vined hope to sow.

So cherish the moments where light starts to beam,
In parched soil, we flourish, excuse the extreme.
For with every struggle, our faith does employ,
In vined hope we thrive, in love, we find joy.

Milton Keynes UK
Ingram Content Group UK Ltd.
UKHW022121021224
451618UK00039B/166